Oils

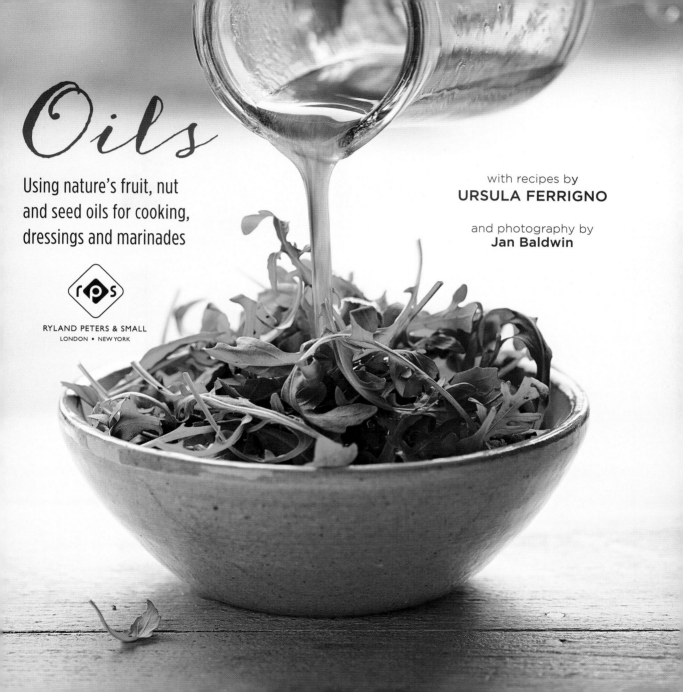

Oils

Using nature's fruit, nut
and seed oils for cooking,
dressings and marinades

with recipes by
URSULA FERRIGNO

and photography by
Jan Baldwin

RYLAND PETERS & SMALL
LONDON • NEW YORK

First published in 2016 by
Ryland Peters & Small
20–21 Jockey's Fields, London
WC1R 4BW
and
341 E 116th St
New York NY 10029

www.rylandpeters.com

10 9 8 7 6 5 4 3 2 1

Please note the recipes in this book
have been previously published
in *The Gourmet Guide to Oil &
Vinegar* by Ursula Ferrigno and
The Perfectly Dressed Salad by
Louise Pickford

ISBN: 978-1-84975-775-1

A CIP record for this book is
available from the British Library.

US Library of Congress cataloguing-in-
publication data has been applied for.

Printed and bound in China

Senior designer Toni Kay
Production controller David Hearn
Art director Leslie Harrington
Editorial director Julia Charles
Publisher Cindy Richards

Prop stylist Jo Harris
Food stylist Emma Marsden
Indexer Hilary Bird

Contents

Introduction

At one time olive oil was simply something that came in bottles from the chemist. It was considered to have medicinal properties but only when applied to the body and was certainly not something anyone would have dreamed of eating! Plenty has changed since those days... Today, modern medical research has confirmed that certain fruit, nut and seed oils have fantastic health-giving benefits and, all around the world, home cooks and professional chefs alike are well aware as to just how versatile and exciting these ingredients culled from natural foods can be.

They can transform a dish into something very special in such an easy, uncomplicated and healthy way. In this book you will learn how something as simple as a slick of fruity extra virgin olive oil over a piece of parchment-baked cod, toasted sesame oil as the base in a sticky Chinese-style five-spice marinade for chicken, or a light walnut oil whisked with vincotto and poured over crisp green salad leaves, can conjure up such stunning results. In addition to the savoury delights you can create, it's also possible to bake cakes and cookies that will satisfy even the sweetest tooth, yet are made using monounsaturated oils, which means that they are no longer loaded with harmful saturated fats. Try sunflower oil baked into a moist banana cake batter or crisp citrusy crackers made with coconut oil for a light-as-air texture.

The variety of oils available for us to buy has never been larger, and each one has its own unique and delicious characteristics. The intention of this book is simply to encourage you to make them your constant culinary companions and enjoy having them as part of your home-cooking repertoire.

Oil directory

As you will no doubt have noticed, a vast variety of different culinary oils are now available to buy. Buy the best you can afford and keep a good range to choose from in your kitchen as they serve myriad purposes – from using in simple salad dressings and marinades, to frying and even baking.

Almond oil

This is a pale, clean oil with a fairly neutral flavour and, rather surprisingly, not much of an almond taste. It is mainly used in baking and confectionery. It can be useful for oiling baking pans or soufflé dishes when making very delicately flavoured batters, or for oiling a marble slab when making sweets/candy. Used alone, it is not enough to give an almond flavour to cakes and biscuits/cookies. For that you need to use almond extract or, of course, almonds themselves.

Argan oil

Argan oil comes from the fruit of the argan tree, native to the Argan forests of Morocco. It is green and fleshy, not unlike a ripe olive. The fleshy part is eaten by the local nimble-footed goats who graze off the trees, digest the fleshy part and after nature takes its course the kernels are collected from the ground and pressed to produce a delicious and distinctive oil. It has a faint reddish tinge and nutty aroma. High in monounsaturated fats, essential fatty acids and antioxidants, it is typically used as a cooking oil in Morocco, to stir into couscous or add a final flourish to tagines (casseroles). It makes a lovely dressing for salads and vegetables or can be mixed with ground almonds and honey to make a delicious spread for hot toast. It's costly as it takes 20 hours to render sufficient nuts to make 1 litre/quart of oil but a little does go a long way!

Avocado oil

The oil of avocados has long been known for its exceptional properties as an ingredient in beauty products, but is now generating excitement in the health and fitness world as it is high in monounsaturated fats and cholesterol-free. It is one of the few fruit oils not derived from the seeds; it is infact pressed from the fleshy pulp surrounding the avocado stone/pit. Extra virgin avocado oil has the characteristically creamy flavour you would expect and an unbelievably high smoke point (250°C/482°F), making it a good choice for healthy frying but it really comes into its own for drizzling and when used in salad dressings. Look for 'Hass' cold-pressed avocado oil, which is a brilliant emerald green when extracted; the colour is attributed to high levels of chlorophylls and carotenoids extracted into the oil. It has been described as having an avocado flavour, with grassy and buttery, mushroom-like notes. Because the avocado is a year-round crop, some olive oil processing facilities, particularly in Australia and New Zealand, process olive oil during the olive season, and avocado oil throughout the rest of the year.

Coconut oil

Coconut oil is in high demand these days but the coconut has long been an important food source for people living in the tropical areas of Asia, Africa, the Pacific and South America. Pressed from the fruit of the coconut palm tree, coconut oil is ideal for light and subtly flavoured dishes. It gives a perfect hint of coconut flavour to Indian and South-east Asian recipes and works well in cakes and desserts. Choose from certified organic, either virgin (unrefined) or refined, depending on your needs and taste. Organic virgin coconut oil has a soft coconut aroma and more pronounced coconut flavour. If you are not keen on the taste or smell of coconut but you want the benefits of the oil, the organic refined version is a better choice. It stands up well to high heat and doesn't add any coconut flavour. Use organic refined coconut oil for

sautéing and stir-frying. If you want to taste the coconut, perhaps in bakes, try virgin or extra-virgin, but take care as it can burn more quickly, making it better suited to medium to low-heat cooking.

Corn/maize oil

This is one of the most economical and widely used of all edible oils. It is extracted from the germ of corn/maize. It is a deep, golden yellow with quite a strong flavour. Refined corn oil has a high smoke point making it a valuable all-purpose frying oil. It is technically suitable for all culinary uses including baking, but is not pleasant in salad dressings and mayonnaise.

Citrus oils

These differ from other culinary oils in that they are used for flavour and not for emulsifying (as in mayonnaise), lubricating (as in salad dressings) or cooking (as in deep-frying). They are extracted from the essential oils stored in the skin of citrus fruits. Grapefruit, lemon and sweet orange oil are remarkable for their aroma and concentration. Just a drop is needed to permeate a dish with the scent and flavour of the fruit. Use them with a dash of gin or vodka to flavour a sauce for fish or chicken dishes. They are delicious stirred into custards or creams for cake filling but less successful added to cake batter since they are so volatile that they simply disappear.

Grapeseed oil

A pale, delicate, quite neutral but pleasant-tasting oil, extracted from grape seeds, that is quite widely available. It is excellent for frying and for general culinary use, and it is a good choice for making mayonnaise. If you want to use hazelnut or sesame oil but find them too strong, then grapeseed oil is excellent for diluting them to your preferred concentration.

Groundnut/peanut oil

This is a clear, pinkish-golden oil made by pressing specially-grown peanuts from Spain, China and India. It is also widely known as groundnut oil. The refined variety has been treated to mellow its strong peanut taste and create a mild-tasting oil with a thin pouring consistency that is suitable for frying and baking as well as in salad dressings and mayonnaise. It is used a great deal in French, South-east Asian and Chinese kitchens. It has a high smoke point and does not burn easily, making it a particularly good choice for wok cooking.

Hazelnut oil

An expensive but delicious oil, this is one of the many nut oils that are now becoming more readily available. Use it on salads, with a little well-aged wine vinegar or lemon juice added, and maybe a few crushed hazelnuts. It is a richly flavoured, nutty brown oil that marries beautifully with fish, for example as a marinade and accompaniment for a raw fish salad. You could also, extravagantly, use it as the shortening when baking with ground hazelnuts. It works very well, but some of the flavour is lost when the oil is heated. However, it has such a powerful flavour to begin with that there is always more than enough left.

Rapeseed/Canola oil
Bright yellow fields of rapeseed produce Britain's only home-grown source of edible oil. It was infact introduced as a crop by the Romans to provide oil, since olives would not grow in Britain. It is a bland, neutrally flavoured oil, suitable for frying, baking and general cookery. It is lower in saturated fats than most other commonly used oils. It is sometimes inaccurately called mustard oil because the rape plant, like mustard, is a member of the brassica family and confusingly has very similar yellow flowers.

Sesame oil
Cold-pressed, unblended sesame oil has a rich, light brown colour, a distinctive smell and a strong, nutty flavour. Indeed, many people find it too strong and so a teaspoon mixed with a couple of tablespoons of grapeseed oil is sufficient. Sesame oil keeps extremely well, since it contains a substance that prevents it from going rancid. Toasted sesame oil, which has a deep golden colour, is an important ingredient in Japanese and Chinese cooking but it is more often used as a flavouring, seasoning or marinating ingredient than as a cooking medium, as the oil burns at a relatively low temperature.

Macadamia oil
Macadamia nuts have grown in Australia's rainforests for thousands of years and were an important food for the Aboriginal tribes. But it took until the 1800s for botanists to discover their potential as a food crop. By this time, they had been transported to Hawaii, which subsequently became the world's largest commercial producer. However, in the 1960s, Australia finally started to grow the trees on a commercial basis and by 1995, production levels had overtaken those of America. Now, areas such as New Zealand, California, Israel and South Africa have also started production. The oil has a slightly sweet flavour. It has a high vitamin and mineral content, oozes with antioxidants, is cholesterol-free and has the highest levels of monounsaturated fats of all the nut and fruit oils, including olive oil. The nuts are sent to a processor and placed into drying bins. After drying, the nuts are cracked and the kernels separated from the shell; they are then mechanically pressed to extract the oil. Macadamia oil has a reasonably high smoke point, and works well in stir-fries, but its fine, buttery flavour is better suited to salads and salsas and to dress white fish and poultry after cooking.

Sunflower oil
Sunflower oil is perhaps the best all-purpose oil. It is tasteless and pale yellow, also light in texture, which makes it excellent for frying, as an ingredient in salad dressings and as the base for mayonnaise, mixed with other more highly flavoured oils if desired.

Pumpkin seed oil
Pumpkins originated in South America and found their way to Europe via America. The plants are only grown as an oil plant in a certain region of Central Europe: a small intersection comprising parts of Austria, Slovenia and Hungary – most of the oil currently comes from Styria, in South-east Austria. The oil is a dark, concentrated green colour and has a velvety texture and intense nutty flavour. It is high in monounsaturated fats, provides an ideal blend of omega-3 and omega-6 oils and is rich in many vital nutrients, including vitamins A and E, selenium and zinc. The seeds are coarsely ground, then toasted before the oil is extracted. It has a fairly low smoke point, so it's best reserved as a salad oil and to drizzle over cooked dishes. It makes a delicious alternative to butter on cooked vegetables, and is excellent drizzled over soups and casseroles.

Walnut oil

This deliciously nutty oil is made in France – in the Dordogne, Périgord and the Loire – and also in Italy. Production is small-scale, and it is therefore an expensive oil. It does not keep too well and once opened it should be stored in a cool place to prevent it from turning rancid. It is wonderful on salads, mixed with only a hint of good vinegar or lemon juice and a few crushed walnuts. It also adds extra depth of flavour in baking. Try it in a walnut and coffee cake, in breakfast breads with a chopped walnut and raisin mixture, in pastry for a walnut tart, or to make walnut biscuits. Mix with lime juice and onions for a marvellous marinade for raw fish. You can also use it to flavour chicken sauces and marinades, and it is delicious with warm vegetables.

Olive oil

This magical oil is now an essential item in everyone's kitchen. There are hundreds of different varieties of olives, and styles of olive oil. Like grapes, the variety grown depends on the climate, the soil and also whether the olives are to be pressed for oil or preserved for eating. With table olives, the firmness and fleshiness of the fruit is of the greatest importance, whereas olives grown for pressing must have a high oil content. All olives are green at first and turn pinky, purpley and then black when fully ripe. Olives flourish in dry, arid conditions. The trees can survive long periods of drought but cannot tolerate extreme cold or damp weather, which is why olives are principally found in Mediterranean climes where the winters tend to be mild. That said, the 'New World' is experiencing a period of growth in its olive oil markets, with Chile, Argentina, South Africa, Australia, New Zealand and the USA at the forefront. South Africa is worth singling out as it has picked up many awards in recent years. Frying with extra virgin olive oil is not recommended, as the heat causes the oil to burn and release free radicals. Also the flavour of the oil is often destroyed, along with the nutritional benefits. There are five grades of olive oil as designated by the International Olive Oil Council:

Extra virgin olive oil
This is virgin olive oil of absolutely perfect taste and odour, having maximum acidity in terms of oleic acid of 1 g per 100 g or with an acidity of less than 1 per cent.

Virgin olive oil
This is virgin oil of absolutely perfect taste and odour, but possessing a maximum acidity in terms of oleic acid of 1.5 g per 100 g or acidity of less than 1.5 per cent

Olive oil
This is the oil mainly used to cook with. It is infact obtained from virgin olive oils by refining methods.

Virgin olive oil lampante (lamp oil)
This is an off-tasting and off-smelling virgin pressing intended for refining or technical purpcses.

Olive residue oil
This is a crude oil obtained by treating olive residues with solvents and is intended for subsequent refining prior to human consumption.

Storing oils

hazelnut oil

sesame oil

chilli/chile-infused oil

sunflower oil

Heat and light both have a degenerative effect on oils. Always buy them in dark glass bottles, cans or ceramic containers. Unlike many wines oils do not grow old gracefully, so do not buy them in bulk unless you use them in very high volume. Ideally, once a bottle of extra virgin olive oil or other high quality culinary oil has been opened, it should be used within 2–3 months.

You may sometimes see olive oil with a white solid layer at the bottom of the bottle. This happens when it has been exposed to the cold and will not damage or change the oil in any way. If a solid layer does form, simply return the oil to room temperature and it will recover. Nevertheless, it's always best not to store any oils for cooking in the refrigerator.

*rapeseed/
canola oil*

walnut oil

*peanut/
groundnut oil*

coconut oil

Dressings

French dressing

1 tablespoon Chardonnay white
   wine vinegar
1 teaspoon Dijon mustard
a pinch of sugar
4 tablespoons extra virgin olive oil
2 tablespoons sunflower oil
salt and pepper

MAKES 100 ML/ABOUT ⅓ CUP

Today the term French dressing is universal but originally it was used to describe a vinaigrette, which is an emulsion of oil and vinegar in varying quantities. To make a really good French dressing the balance of flavours should be just right – neither too sharp nor too oily. This recipe ticks all the boxes.

In a bowl stir together the vinegar, mustard, sugar, salt and pepper until smooth and then gradually whisk in the oils until amalgamated. Season to taste and serve. Alternatively store in a screw top jar in the fridge for up to 1 week, shaking well before use. Use on any salad of your choice.

Tarragon vinaigrette

2 teaspoons white wine vinegar
   or tarragon vinegar
1 teaspoon Dijon mustard
½–1 teaspoon caster/superfine sugar
2 tablespoons chopped fresh
   tarragon
3 tablespoons macadamia or
   hazelnut oil
1 tablespoon extra virgin olive oil
salt and pepper

MAKES 125 ML/½ CUP

When available, use macadamia nut oil in this dressing as it has a mild nutty flavour that really shows off the tarragon to its best. Hazelnut oil is also good and perhaps a more readily available alternative. If you love the flavour of tarragon, use tarragon vinegar.

Place the vinegar, mustard, sugar, tarragon and a little salt and pepper in a blender and blend until combined, then add the oil and blend again until amalgamated. Adjust seasoning to taste and serve.

Serve this dressing over a poached salmon salad.

Walnut and vincotto dressing

1 tablespoon vincotto
2 teaspoons red wine vinegar
3 tablespoons walnut oil
1 tablespoon extra virgin olive oil
salt and pepper

MAKES 75 ML/⅓ CUP

Vincotto (cooked wine) is a sweet, dark syrup made from fermented grape must and comes from Apulia in the south of Italy. It is available from Italian delis and specialist food stores.

Whisk all the ingredients together, adjust seasoning to taste and serve. Serve drizzled over a tomato and rocket/arugula salad with shavings of aged Parmesan.

Sherry, orange and raisin dressing

2 tablespoons extra virgin olive oil
30 g/1 oz. blanched whole
    hazelnuts
30 g/1 oz. raisins
3 tablespoons Pedro Ximenez,
    sweet sherry or raisin juice
2 tablespoons sherry vinegar
grated zest and juice 1 orange,
    about 3½ tablespoons
4 tablespoons hazelnut oil
salt and pepper

MAKES 200 ML/ABOUT 1 CUP

Pedro Ximenez is an intensely sweet dessert sherry made from grapes grown throughout Spain. In South America it is known as Pedro Gimenez. If unavailable, you could use Marsala or an alcohol-free alternative, such as raisin juice.

Heat the olive oil in a frying pan/skillet and gently fry the hazelnuts for 1–2 minute until golden, add the raisins and fry for a further 1 minute until soft.

Add the sherry and sherry vinegar to the pan and bubble for 30 seconds. Whisk in the orange zest and juice and warm through, then remove from the heat and transfer to a bowl.

Gradually whisk in the hazelnut oil, season to taste and serve warm with a salad of duck, chicory/endive and orange segments.

Sweet chilli

75 ml/⅓ cup rice wine vinegar
50 g/¼ cup granulated sugar
2 red bird's eye chillies/chiles,
  thinly sliced
6 tablespoons peanut oil
freshly squeezed juice ½ lime
2 tablespoons Thai fish sauce
salt

MAKES 150 ML/⅔ CUP

Hot, sweet and sour together is a flavour combination we associate with Asian cuisine and this dressing epitomizes that. Using bird's eye chillies/chiles will result in a fiery dressing so, if you prefer a milder heat, discard the seeds.

Place the vinegar, sugar and 1 tablespoon water in a small saucepan and heat gently to dissolve the sugar, then simmer for 5 minutes until the mixture is syrupy. Stir in the sliced chillies/chiles and allow to cool completely.

Whisk in the remaining ingredients until the dressing is amalgamated and adjust seasoning to taste.

This is wonderful drizzled over a Thai beef salad with tomatoes, cucumber, red onions and fresh herbs.

Coriander and toasted sesame

2 tablespoons sesame seeds
2 large spring onions/scallions,
  trimmed and chopped
1 tablespoon chopped coriander/
  cilantro leaves
1 teaspoon caster/superfine sugar
1 tablespoon rice wine vinegar
1 tablespoon light soy sauce
3 tablespoons sunflower oil
2 teaspoons sesame oil
salt and pepper

MAKES 150 ML/⅔ CUP

The toasted sesame seeds add a wonderfully nutty, smoky flavour to this Japanese-style dressing. It is delicious tossed through any noodle and crispy vegetable salad. If making ahead, make sure to give it a really good shake before using. This dressing is similar to the traditional Japanese dressing served over wilted spinach.

Dry fry the sesame seeds in a small fry pan over a medium heat until toasted and starting to release their aroma. Cool and transfer to a blender. Blend to a paste with the spring onions/scallions, coriander/cilantro, sugar, vinegar, soy sauce and a pinch of salt.

Add the oils and blend again until amalgamated. Adjust seasoning to taste and serve.

Wasabi, lemon and avocado oil

1 teaspoon wasabi paste
½ teaspoon caster/superfine sugar
1 tablespoon freshly squeezed
   lemon or lime juice
3 tablespoons avocado oil
a pinch of salt

MAKES 75 ML/⅓ CUP

Wasabi is Japanese horseradish, an integral ingredient in sushi and an accompaniment to sashimi. It adds a wonderful pungency to dishes and is lovely in a salad dressing. Rather than combining it with other traditional Japanese ingredients, here it is whisked with avocado oil and lemon juice for a refreshingly different flavour.

Place the wasabi paste, sugar, lemon or lime juice and the salt in a bowl and, using a small balloon whisk, blend to form a smooth paste. Gradually whisk in the oil until amalgamated and adjust seasoning to taste.

This is delicious drizzled over raw tuna or beef carpaccio or a cooked prawn/shrimp salad.

Mirin

50 ml/3½ tablespoons mirin
1 spring onion/scallion, trimmed
   and thinly sliced
1 garlic clove, sliced
2 tablespoons rice wine vinegar
1 tablespoon dark soy sauce
2 tablespoons peanut or sunflower
   oil
1 tablespoon chopped fresh
   coriander/cilantro

MAKES 150 ML/⅔ CUP

This is a mildly flavoured Japanese-style dressing with a little sweetness from the mirin, balanced beautifully with the rice wine vinegar. It is lovely served warm poured over oysters on the half shell or over grilled scallops.

Place the mirin, half the spring onion/scallion, the garlic, vinegar and soy sauce in a small saucepan. Bring to the boil and simmer gently for 2 minutes. Strain the liquid through a sieve/strainer and set aside to cool to slightly.

Whisk in the oil, stir in the chopped coriander/cilantro and remaining spring onion/scallion and serve immediately.

Mexican lime, coriander and chipotle

1–2 teaspoons dried chipotle chilli/
   chile paste
grated zest and freshly squeezed
   juice 1 lime
1 teaspoon agave syrup
3 tablespoons pumpkin seed oil
   or avocado oil
1 tablespoon chopped fresh
   coriander/cilantro
salt and pepper

MAKES 75 ML/⅓ CUP

Chipotle chillies/chiles have a wonderfully smoky flavour and aroma, giving this dressing a wonderful rich quality. You can buy dried chipotle chillies/chiles if you prefer but the paste, available from specialist food stores, is perfect for dressings. Both agave syrup and pumpkin seed oil will be available in health food stores.

Combine the chilli/chile paste, lime zest and juice, agave syrup and a little salt and pepper in a bowl and whisk until smooth. Gradually whisk in the oil until smooth, stir in the coriander/cilantro and serve.

Try drizzling this dressing over a shredded chicken, corn and avocado salad on a warm tortilla.

Key West mango and lime

flesh of 1 small ripe mango, diced
grated zest and freshly squeezed
   juice 2 small limes
2 teaspoons clear honey
3 tablespoons avocado oil
1 red chilli/chile, seeded and
   finely chopped
salt and pepper

MAKES 150 ML/⅔ CUP

Mango flesh provides a great base for this pretty dressing, but you will need to buy a ripe mango. The dressing is perfect for serving with cooked prawns/shrimp and would make a great alternative sauce for a prawn/shrimp cocktail with avocado and lettuce.

Place the mango in a blender with the lime zest, juice, honey and a little salt and pepper and blend until smooth, add the oil and blend again. Transfer to a bowl and stir in the chilli/chile. Adjust seasoning to taste and serve.

Moroccan spice

5 tablespoons argan or olive oil
½ small onion, thinly sliced
1 garlic clove, crushed
1 teaspoon Ras al Hanout (Moroccan spice mix)
2 teaspoons pomegranate molasses
½ teaspoon clear honey
1 tablespoon finely sliced preserved lemon
1 tablespoon red wine vinegar
salt and pepper

MAKES 150 ML/⅔ CUP

This dressing uses Argan oil with a hot-sweet Moroccan spice blend which can typically contain a range of ingredients from ground coriander and fenugreek through to kaffir lime and rose petals. Try it poured over a chickpea salad with shredded chicken, raisins, toasted almonds and chopped fresh herbs.

Heat 2 tablespoons of the oil in a small frying pan/skillet and gently fry the onion, garlic, spice mix and a little salt and pepper over a low heat for 5 minutes. Stir in the pomegranate molasses and honey and warm through. Remove the pan from the heat and whisk in the remaining oil. Stir in the preserved lemon and adjust seasoning to taste.

Serve immediately.

Preserved lemon

4 tablespoons extra virgin olive oil
1 tablespoon finely diced preserved lemon
1 garlic clove, crushed
1 tablespoon freshly squeezed lemon juice
2 teaspoons clear honey
1 tablespoon chopped fresh coriander/cilantro
salt and pepper

MAKES 150 ML/⅔ CUP

This salty-sour dressing with a hint of sweetness is a real winner and is fantastic served with a crisp green leaf salad or stirred through a chicken couscous salad. Preserved lemons are now readily available and should be found in larger supermarkets; alternatively try Middle Eastern food stores and delis.

Combine all the ingredients in a blender and blend until smooth and vibrant green.

Drizzle over a salad of couscous, shredded grilled/broiled chicken, tomatoes and fresh spring onions/scallions.

Simple herb infused oils

Herb oils are simple to make. Particularly lovely oils can be made using basil, rosemary, tarragon and thyme. Crush the herbs using a pestle and mortar then put 2 tablespoons of the crushed herbs into a 300-ml/10-fl. oz. bottle. Add olive oil, filling the bottle three-quarters full. Add 1 tablespoon of wine vinegar and cork the bottle tightly. Put the bottle into a double boiler and 'cook' it at just below boiling point for a few hours each day for a week. When the oil is ready, add a sprig of the dried herb to the bottle for decoration.

Saffron oil

a large pinch of saffron strands
1 tablespoon white wine vinegar
1 teaspoon caster/superfine sugar
4 tablespoons extra virgin olive oil
salt and pepper

MAKES 100 ML/⅓ CUP

The saffron adds both a pretty colour and a delightfully delicate flavour to the dressing, which is delicious when drizzled over a mixed leaf and tomato salad.

Place the saffron, 1 tablespoon water, vinegar and sugar in a small saucepan and heat gently, stirring until the sugar is dissolved. Bring to the boil and remove from the heat. Set aside to cool completely.

Add the oil, season to taste and serve.

Basil oil

25 g/¾ oz. fresh basil leaves
300 ml/1¼ cup extra virgin olive oil
a little freshly squeezed lemon juice
a pinch of salt

MAKES 100 ML/⅓ CUP

This dressing is fragrant with pungent fresh basil leaves. It is best made in the summer months when basil is at its prime and, of course, most inexpensive.

Blend the basil leaves, oil and a little salt in a blender to make a vivid green paste. Allow to infuse overnight and the next day strain the oil through a layer of muslin/cheesecloth. Store the oil in the fridge, returning to room temperature before use.

This dressing is best served with lemon juice but, rather than mixing the juice into the oil, add it directly to the salad.

Bay and thyme

6 bay leaves
4 sprigs fresh thyme
salt and pepper
150 ml/⅔ cup extra virgin
  olive oil
1–2 tablespoons vinegar of your
  choice

MAKES 200 ML/1 SCANT CUP

Bay and thyme give the oil a mellow flavour and, once strained, it is perfectly enhanced with a light vinegar, such as Chinese black vinegar or rice wine vinegar.

Place the bay leaves, thyme, salt and pepper in a pestle and mortar and pound gently to bash up the herbs. Transfer to a jar, add the oil and marinate for 5 days.

Strain the oil into a jar, add vinegar, salt and pepper to taste and serve.

This dressing is great served over salad leaves or shaved courgettes/zucchini.

Smoked garlic oil

8 tablespoons soft brown sugar
8 tablespoons long grain rice
8 tablespoons tea leaves
1 head garlic
250 ml/1 cup plus 1 tablespoon
  extra virgin olive
freshly squeezed lemon juice,
  to taste
salt and pepper

MAKES 300 ML/1¼ CUPS

Tea-smoking is a terrific way to flavour foods. It is often used to smoke salmon or duck, but works well here with the garlic. You will need to double line the wok with foil and open a window when you are smoking foods as the aroma is quite pungent.

Line a wok with a double sheet of foil and combine the brown sugar, rice and tea leaves in the bottom. Place a small rack or griddle over the smoking mixture (making sure the two don't touch) and lay the garlic on the rack.

Place the wok over a high heat and, as soon as the mixture starts to smoke, top the wok with a tight-fitting lid. Lower the heat and cook gently for 15 minutes until the garlic turns a deep brown. Allow to cool.

Place the unpeeled garlic in a bottle or jar, add the oil and allow to infuse for 1 week. Drain and use the oil to make a dressing, adding vinegar or lemon juice to taste. Great with a beef carpaccio or a charred lamb salad.

Meat and Poultry

Carpaccio with gorgonzola and walnuts

750 g/1 lb. 10 oz. beef fillet,
   tail end in one piece
200 g/7 oz. rocket/arugula
200 g/7 oz. aged Gorgonzola
   Piccante, crumbled
85 g/²/₃ cup coarsely chopped
   fresh walnuts
a handful of flat-leaf parsley,
   roughly chopped
4–6 tablespoons fruity
   extra virgin olive oil
sea salt and freshly ground
   black pepper
2 unwaxed lemons, halved,
   to serve

SERVES 4

This is my improvisation on the classic recipe and is very easy to prepare.
Be sure to use prime ingredients, particularly when it comes to the beef.

Wrap the beef in clingfilm/plastic wrap and place in the freezer for 2 hours (this makes it easier to slice). Remove the plastic and, using a sharp filleting knife, cut the beef into paper-thin slices.

Cover four individual plates with the carpaccio slices. Rinse the rocket/arugula and place a mound on top. Sprinkle with the cheese, walnuts and parsley. Drizzle with the oil and season. Serve with the lemon halves for squeezing over.

Sweet and sour spare ribs

2 kg/4½ lbs. pork spare ribs
sea salt
2 tablespoons groundnut/peanut oil

FOR THE SAUCE:
2 tablespoons groundnut/peanut oil
1 large onion, finely chopped
1 large garlic clove, crushed
1 tablespoon cider vinegar
1 tablespoon tomato purée/paste
1 tablespoon tamari soy sauce
4 teaspoons soft light brown sugar
1 tablespoon clear honey
300ml/1¼ cups fresh chicken stock
freshly squeezed juice of 1 lemon
freshly ground black pepper
sticky white rice, to serve (optional)

SERVES 6–8

This recipe has special memories for me. My mother made this when we were teenagers for family parties and gatherings. We were always eating Italian food, and when she produced this dish, we thought we were so exotic!

Preheat the oven to 190°C (375°F) Gas 5. Sprinkle the pork with salt to taste and place in a roasting pan. Pour over the oil and roast for 25 minutes.

Remove the pork from the oven and use a sharp knife to cut it into individual ribs.

To prepare the sauce, heat 1 tablespoon of the oil in a small pan, add the onion and cook gently until coloured. Add the garlic and cook gently. Add all the remaining sauce ingredients, along with pepper to taste. Mix well.

Return the meat to the roasting pan, pour over the sauce and continue to roast, covered with foil, for 1–1½ hours. Serve with rice or your favourite accompaniment.

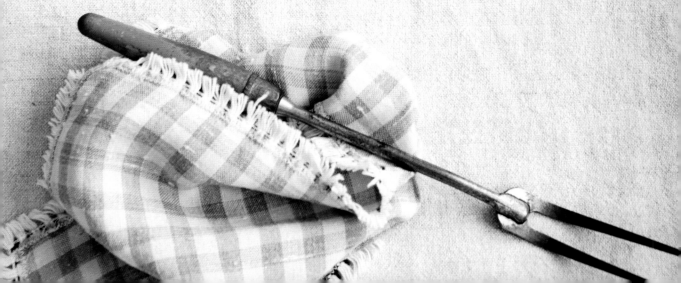

Pork roast braised with milk and fresh herbs

50 ml/3 tablespoons olive oil

2–2.25-kg/4½–5-lb. boneless pork shoulder roast (without skin), tied

3 juniper berries, crushed (see Cook's notes)

2 large sprigs of fresh rosemary

2 large sprigs of fresh sage

1 sprig of fresh or 4 dried bay leaves

1 garlic clove

fine sea salt and freshly ground black pepper

50 ml/3 tablespoons white wine vinegar

1 litre/1 quart whole milk

SERVES 6–8

Simmering a pork roast with milk and a generous handful of herbs results in very tender meat with rich silky juices. Many Italians will leave the milk curds that form alongside the meat where they are, but I strain them out for a more refined sauce.

Preheat the oven to 180°C (350°F) Gas 4 with the shelf/rack in the middle of the oven.

Heat the oil in a large, wide ovenproof heavy saucepan over a medium heat, then lightly brown the pork on all sides with the juniper berries and herbs for 8–10 minutes in total.

Add the garlic clove and sprinkle the pork with 1 teaspoon fine sea salt and ½ teaspoon black pepper. Cook until the garlic is golden, about 1 minute. Pour the white wine vinegar over the roast and briskly simmer until it is reduced by half.

Pour the milk over the roast and bring to a bare simmer. Cover the saucepan and braise the pork in the oven, turning it occasionally, for 2–2½ hours until tender (the milk will form curds).

Transfer the roast to a carving board and loosely cover. Strain the juices through a fine-mesh sieve/strainer into a bowl (discard the solids) and skim off the fat. Return the juices to the saucepan and boil until flavourful and reduced to about 450 ml/2 cups. Season to taste with salt and pepper.

Slice the pork and serve it moistened with the juices.

Cook's notes: Juniper berries can be found in the spice aisle at supermarkets. The pork can be braised a day ahead and chilled in the liquid, uncovered, until cool, then covered. Bring to room temperature, then reheat and proceed with the recipe.

Salmoriglio lamb with borlotti and green bean salad

5 garlic cloves, 4 crushed

1 tablespoon chilli/hot red pepper flakes

3 tablespoons light brown sugar

thickly grated zest and freshly squeezed juice of 2 lemons

a small handful of oregano leaves, chopped

100 ml/6 tablespoons extra virgin olive oil

2-kg/4½-lbs. butterflied leg of lamb

sea salt and freshly ground black pepper

FOR THE SALAD:

3 red onions, thickly sliced

light brown sugar, to taste

3 tablespoons balsamic vinegar

2 x 400-g/14-oz. cans borlotti beans, drained and rinsed

300 g/11 oz. small vine-ripened tomatoes, halved

100 g/3½ oz. green beans, blanched

15 black olives, stoned/pitted

SERVES 6

Salmoriglio is a Sicilian sauce of oregano and olive oil used for marinating fish and meat, or to dress a salad. Here it is used to marinate then lamb and then doubles up as a delicious salad dressing.

Make the marinade by mixing the 4 crushed garlic cloves, the chilli/hot red pepper flakes, brown sugar, lemon zest, three-quarters of the lemon juice, half the oregano and 2 tablespoons of the olive oil in a small bowl. Season the meat all over and lay it in a glass ovenproof dish. Pour over the marinade and massage it into the lamb. Cover with clingfilm/plastic wrap and refrigerate overnight or for at least 2 hours. Bring back to room temperature before cooking.

Preheat the oven to 180°C (350°F) Gas 4. Arrange the onion slices in a large roasting pan. Season well and drizzle with some of the remaining olive oil, a little sugar and the balsamic vinegar. Roast for 30 minutes and then remove from the oven. Put the borlotti beans in a dish and top with the tomatoes, green beans, olives and onions.

Chop the remaining oregano and garlic clove until very fine. Put in a bowl with some seasoning and the lemon juice.

Heat a barbecue/gas or charcoal grill. Cook the lamb for 15 minutes on each side on indirect heat for pink meat. Leave to rest for 10 minutes. If cooking indoors, chargrill or sear the lamb in a hot griddle/grill pan or frying pan/skillet until browned on both sides, then finish in a preheated 200°C (400°F) Gas 6 oven for 25–30 minutes. Serve the meat sliced with the salad and a bowl of the oregano sauce.

Sweet, sticky Chinese chicken

4 Maryland pieces of chicken
(leg and thigh together)

FOR THE MARINADE:
grated zest and juice of 1 orange
3 tablespoons clear honey
2 tablespoons muscovado/
    light brown sugar
1 tablespoon Chinese five-spice
    powder
2 tablespoons soy sauce
2 tablespoons toasted sesame oil
crisp green salad, to serve

SERVES 8

As an Italian, I love Italian food. However, as I live with a gourmet husband whose palate extends across the globe, I sometimes have to step outside Italy. This easy, home-from-work recipe fits the bill.

Put the chicken in a sealable plastic bag. Mix all the marinade ingredients together and pour over the chicken. Seal the bag and squidge it together to coat the chicken well. Refrigerate for at least 2 hours (overnight is better).

Preheat the oven to 180°C (350°F) Gas 4. Tip the chicken and marinade into a large roasting tin and spread it out evenly. Roast for 45 minutes until the chicken is cooked through with no pink meat, and the juices run clear.

Remove the cooked chicken from the oven and, if liked, finish in a hot griddle/grill pan, browning the pieces skin-side down for about 5 minutes until the chicken is crisp and slightly charred. Serve with a crisp salad.

Marinated duck breasts with cucumber and mint salad

2 duck breasts
125 g/4½ oz. cucumber, sliced
   in matchsticks
1 teaspoon sea salt
1 red onion, finely chopped
2 tablespoons white wine vinegar
1 tablespoon rapeseed/canola oil
2 tablespoons fruity extra virgin
   olive oil
1 tablespoon caster/granulated
   sugar
a large handful of mint leaves,
   stalks removed and chopped
a 110-g/4-oz. bag pea shoots

FOR THE MARINADE:
1 cinnamon stick
1 star anise
2 teaspoons coriander seeds
3-cm/1¼-in. piece of fresh ginger,
   peeled and finely grated
2 shallots, finely diced
1 tablespoon sea salt
3 tablespoons rice vinegar

SERVES 4

This recipe is fairly demanding in terms of ingredients and effort, but it is well worth it! The combination of Asian flavours is very authentic, making the dish a perennial hit with the family and dinner guests alike.

To make the marinade, dry roast the spices in a frying pan/skillet for 1½–2 minutes until fragrant, then pound in a pestle and mortar with the ginger and shallots. Mix in the salt and rice vinegar, then rub over the duck breasts in a glass dish. Cover with clingfilm/plastic wrap and refrigerate for a minimum of 2 hours or overnight if possible.

For the salad, toss the cucumber with 1 teaspoon salt in a colander. Drain in the sink for 20 minutes. Scatter the cucumber slices on paper towels and pat dry. Soak the red onion in cold water for 10 minutes, then drain.

Mix the cucumber, red onion, vinegar, oils, sugar and mint together in a bowl. Season with salt and pepper, and set aside.

Preheat the oven to 180°C (350°C) Gas 4. Brush the marinade off the duck breasts and place skin-side down in a cold, ovenproof frying pan/skillet. Cook over a medium heat for 15 minutes, and pour away any excess fat.

Turn the breasts over and cook for 2 minutes, then place in the oven for 10 minutes.

Slice the duck and serve with the cucumber salad, with the pea shoots mixed in.

Fish and Seafood

Asian-style salt and pepper shrimp

4 tablespoons cornflour/
  cornstarch
4 teaspoons fine sea salt
2 teaspoons freshly ground
  black pepper
1½ teaspoons Chinese five-spice
  powder
1 kg/2¼ lbs. raw king prawns/
  jumbo shrimp, peeled and
  deveined
150 ml/⅔ cup sunflower or
  groundnut/peanut oil
1 medium fresh red chilli/chile
a handful of fresh coriander/
  cilantro or flat-leaf parsley,
  to garnish
lemon wedges, to serve

SERVES 4–6

Deliciously straightforward, this makes a super starter for informal suppers. Serve freshly cooked, garnished with crispy fried chilli/chiles and lemons for squeezing.

Mix the cornflour/cornstarch, salt, pepper and five-spice on a large plate. Dust the prawns/shrimp in the seasoned cornflour/cornstarch and shake off any excess. Place a wok or similar vessel on a medium-high heat, add the oil and heat until smoking.

Fry the prawns/shrimp in batches for about 2 minutes until golden and crisp, turning halfway through cooking. Drain the prawns/shrimp on paper towels and keep them warm.

Fry the chilli/chile for a few seconds after you have cooked the prawns/shrimp. Serve with the fried chilli/chile and lemon slices, garnished with the coriander/cilantro or parsley, and more seasoning if you like.

Black cod with olives and potatoes in parchment

250 g/9 oz. small new potatoes

3 tablespoons plus 1 teaspoon olive oil

1 tablespoon plus 2 teaspoons finely chopped fresh oregano leaves

2¼ teaspoons fine sea salt

8 x 150-g/5½-oz. pieces skinless black cod, Pacific cod or haddock fillet (about 2.5 cm/ 1 in. thick), any bones removed

1 lemon, very thinly sliced

6 garlic cloves, thinly sliced

125 g/1 cup Kalamata black olives, pitted and slivered

a handful of fresh flat-leaf parsley

delicate extra virgin olive oil, for drizzling

baking parchment

kitchen string/twine

SERVES 8

A favourite Barese recipe (often named after San Nicola, the guardian saint of sailors), these little packets seal in the fish and vegetable juices, with the potato slices insulating the fish from the heat of the oven. The olives and lemon slices emphasize the bright flavours of the dish.

Preheat the oven to 200°C (400°F) Gas 6, and heat a baking sheet on the bottom shelf/rack.

Carefully cut the potatoes into very thin slices using a sharp knife. Toss the potatoes with 2 tablespoons of the oil, 1 teaspoon oregano and ¼ teaspoon sea salt. Divide the potatoes among 8 large squares of baking parchment, arranging them in the centre so that they overlap slightly, then top with a piece of fish.

Sprinkle each fillet with a scant ¼ teaspoon sea salt, then top each with a lemon slice, a few garlic and olive slivers, parsley, ½ teaspoon oregano and ½ teaspoon oil.

Gather the sides of the parchment up and over the fish to form a pouch, leaving no openings, and tie tightly with kitchen string. Put the packages on the hot baking sheet and bake in the preheated oven until the fish is just cooked through, 15–22 minutes.

Cut open the parchment parcels to serve and drizzle with the extra virgin olive oil.

Swordfish skewers with walnut sauce

1 kg/2¼ lbs. swordfish (or any other firm white fish), skinned and cut into 4-cm/2-in. cubes

grated zest and freshly squeezed juice of 2 lemons

175 ml/¾ cup olive oil

a handful of fresh mint leaves, finely chopped

sea salt and freshly ground black pepper

a large handful of fresh bay leaves

2 lemons, cut into wedges

FOR THE WALNUT SAUCE:

125 g/1¼ cups fresh walnut halves

1 large garlic clove

160 ml/⅔ cup walnut oil

1 slice white or brown sourdough bread, soaked in water and then squeezed dry

freshly squeezed juice of 1 lemon

sea salt and freshly ground black pepper

a baking sheet lined with parchment paper

6 metal or wood kebab/kabob skewers (soaked in water if wooden)

SERVES 6

Swordfish and mint are firm favourites as a flavour combination, and the creamy walnut sauce is simply delicious. This is perfect summer food.

To make the walnut sauce, preheat the oven to 200°C (400°F) Gas 6. Toast the walnuts on the prepared baking sheet for 8 minutes.

Grind the walnuts in a food processor (or using a pestle and mortar) with the garlic, oil, bread and the lemon juice. You should have a thick, smooth sauce. Adjust the seasoning to taste. Cover and set aside until ready to serve.

Put the swordfish cubes, lemon zest and juice, olive oil, mint and salt and pepper in a large bowl. Mix to coat, cover with clingfilm/plastic wrap and leave in the fridge for a minimum of 1 hour.

Remove the fish from the marinade and thread onto the skewers, alternating with bay leaves and lemon wedges.

Cook under a preheated medium grill/broiler, turning after 10 minutes and brushing with the marinade. Alternatively, cook on a hot barbecue/gas or charcoal grill for 6 minutes, brushing with the marinade.

Mackerel with apple, watercress and ajo blanco

6 fresh mackerel fillets, skin scored
1 tablespoon olive oil
3 crisp, sweet red apples, cored
    and thinly sliced
150 g/5½ oz. watercress
2 tablespoons red wine vinegar
1 small red onion, thinly sliced into
    half moons, to garnish
freshly squeezed juice, to taste
sea salt and freshly ground
    black pepper

FOR THE AJO BLANCO:
50 g/1¾ oz. stale white bread,
    crusts removed (sourdough
    is best)
125 g/1 cup blanched white almonds
1 garlic clove, chopped
1 tablespoon white balsamic vinegar
2 tablespoons Spanish extra virgin
    olive oil

SERVES 6

This is a fine combination of flavours. I first demonstrated this recipe at a farm called Burwash Manor, near Cambridge, England. It was their annual Apple Day and the response was very encouraging!

To make the ajo blanco, soak the bread in a bowl with cold water for 15 minutes. Finely grind the almonds in a food processor. Pour 100 ml/ scant ½ cup of cold water into the processor and blend until you have a loose paste. Add the garlic and blend. Drain the bread and add to the almond paste mixture along with the vinegar and extra virgin olive oil. Season to taste with salt and pepper. Cover and transfer to the fridge for at least 1 hour.

Heat a griddle/grill pan or heavy frying pan/skillet until hot. Brush the mackerel with the oil and season. Cook the fillets skin-side down in the hot pan for 4 minutes then turn and cook for a further 2 minutes on the other side.

Put the apple slices and watercress in a bowl, add the red wine vinegar and toss until coated. Arrange the salad mixture on serving plates. Place a mackerel fillet on each one, squeeze over a little lemon juice and top with slices of red onion. Serve the ajo blanco on the side.

Sicilian-style tuna with fennel and chillies

4 x 125-g/4-oz. fresh tuna steaks
2 fennel bulbs, thinly sliced
    through the root
2 red onions, sliced
2–3 tablespoons olive oil
crusty bread, to serve

FOR THE MARINADE:
125 ml/½ cup Sicilian extra
    virgin olive oil
4 fresh red chillies/chiles,
    deseeded and finely chopped
4 garlic cloves, crushed
grated zest and freshly
    squeezed juice of 3 lemons
a large handful of fresh flat-leaf
    parsley, finely chopped
sea salt and freshly ground
    black pepper

SERVES 4

My lasting memories of Sicily are travelling on a business trip with my father. Business was conducted not in an office restaurant but in a fish market, then in the car, and then in the kitchen where this dish was prepared for us. I shall never forget this lunch. I experienced such convivial hospitality and memorable food that I have now written about it in two books.

To make the marinade, mix all the ingredients together in a bowl and season to taste with salt and pepper.

Place the tuna steaks in a shallow non-reactive dish and cover with 2–3 spoonfuls of the marinade. Reserve the remaining marinade.

Place a griddle/grill pan or heavy frying pan/skillet over medium heat. Toss the fennel and onions with the oil, then cook in the pan for 5 minutes on each side to soften. Transfer to a plate and drizzle with the reserved marinade.

Remove the tuna from the marinade and add to the hot pan. Cook for 4–5 minutes on each side, until cooked to your liking.

Serve the tuna steaks on the vegetables with some crusty bread to mop up the juices.

Vegetables

Radiccho, endive & pear salad with Provolone and walnuts

100 g/1 cup fresh walnut halves
1 head chicory/Belgian endive
½ head radicchio
a handful of fresh basil leaves, torn
a handful of fresh mint leaves, chopped
125 g/4½ oz. pea shoots
2 large, ripe but firm pears
150 g/5½ oz. Provolone cheese, cut into triangles

FOR THE VINAIGRETTE:
1 tablespoon red wine vinegar
2 teaspoons aged balsamic vinegar
3 tablespoons walnut oil
1 tablespoon olive oil
sea salt and freshly ground black pepper

SERVES 4–5

Provolone is a cow's milk cheese from Italy's southern region. It has a slightly smoky flavour and fine texture. The colour is pale yellow when aged between 2 and 3 months, but as the cheese ripens, the colour and flavour deepen. A mature goats' cheese would also work very well.

Preheat the oven to 180°C (350°F) Gas 4. Spread the walnuts on a baking sheet and bake them for 10 minutes until they are fragrant. Let cool before roughly chopping.

Next, make the vinaigrette. Combine the salt, red wine vinegar and balsamic vinegar in a bowl and whisk until the salt has dissolved. Trickle in the two types of oil, whisking all the while until the mixture has emulsified. Season to taste with pepper.

Separate the chicory/endive and radicchio leaves, rinse well and pat dry. Place in a bowl with the herbs and pea shoots. Add 2 tablespoons of the vinaigrette and toss well, then use to make a bed on a plate.

Quarter and core the pears, then arrange them on top of the leaves with the cheese and walnuts. Drizzle with the dressing and serve straight away.

Sweet & sour peppers with mozzarella

3 x 125-g/4½-oz. balls fresh buffalo
   mozzarella, sliced
6 Queen Spanish or other large
   green olives, stoned/pitted and
   sliced lengthways
60 g/2¼ oz. rocket/arugula
1 tablespoon extra virgin olive oil
   (light and not too bold)
crusty bread, to serve

FOR THE PEPPERS:
6 (bell) peppers, a mixture of red,
   yellow and orange
3 tablespoons white wine vinegar
6 tablespoons fruity extra virgin
   olive oil (Ligurian is best here)
50 g/⅓ cup sultanas/golden raisins
1½ teaspoons cumin seeds
1 teaspoon crushed dried red chilli/
   hot pepper flakes
sea salt and freshly ground
   black pepper
1 garlic clove, finely sliced
2 teaspoons caster/granulated
   sugar

*a baking sheet, lined with baking
   parchment*

SERVES 4–6

This antipasto is timeless and its colour, simplicity and flavour always hit the right key. It is ideal for those with busy lives, as it can be made days in advance. There was always some roasted pepper in my Nonna's kitchen to dip crusty bread into as a wonderful healthy snack.

Preheat the oven to 200°C (400°F) Gas 6.

Place the peppers on the prepared baking sheet and roast in the preheated oven for 25 minutes until slightly blackened and deflated. Leave to cool. Peel the peppers and discard the seeds, then cut the flesh into 1-cm/½-in. strips. Mix the pepper strips with the vinegar, oil, sultanas/golden raisins, cumin and pepper flakes. Season to taste. Add the garlic and sugar and leave to infuse.

To serve, divide the mozzarella between serving plates, spoon over the pepper mixture and scatter over the olives. Toss the rocket/arugula leaves in the oil and scatter some on each plate. Serve immediately.

Asian-style carrot salad with ginger

This salad is full of history for me. As a very young cookery teacher, I used to demonstrate this dish regularly. I love its colours and crunch factor. Providing your store cupboard is well stocked, this salad can be made quickly and easily.

30 g/¼ cup pumpkin seeds
6 tablespoons tamari soy sauce
4 medium organic carrots,
   cut into matchsticks
150 g/5½ oz. pea shoots
3 spring onions/scallions,
   sliced at an angle

FOR THE GINGER DRESSING:
1-cm/½-in. piece of fresh ginger,
   peeled and finely grated
2 tablespoons mirin
   (sweetened rice wine)
1 tablespoon rice vinegar
2 tablespoons toasted sesame oil
sea salt and freshly ground
   black pepper

SERVES 4–6

Dry-fry the pumpkin seeds in a frying pan/skillet, constantly tosssing the pan to prevent the seeds from burning. Once they start to colour, turn off the heat, add 4 tablespoons of the tamari and stir to combine. Leave them to cool and go crunchy.

To make the ginger dressing, combine the ingredients in a jam jar with a screwtop lid. Season to taste with salt and pepper. Shake well and set aside until needed.

Combine the carrots, pea shoots and spring onions/scallions. Sprinkle over the crunchy pumpkin seeds. Shake the dressing, pour it over the salad and serve immediately.

Leek and chickpeas with mustard dressing

5 tablespoons rapeseed/
  canola oil

4 medium leeks, washed well
  and finely chopped

sea salt

400 g/2 cups cooked chickpeas
  (1/3 crushed if liked to absorb
  more flavour)

a handful of fresh flat-leaf
  parsley, finely chopped

3 teaspoons freshly ground
  black pepper

1 tablespoon Dijon mustard

1 teaspoon wholegrain mustard

1 tablespoon white wine vinegar

SERVES 4–6

This is a relaxed dish to serve with meat or fish, or as an appetizer with sourdough on the side. It improves in flavour over time, so it's a good idea to make it in advance.

Heat 2 tablespoons of the oil in a frying pan/skillet, add the leeks and salt to taste and cook until softened. Add the chickpeas, mix well and heat well together. Take off the heat and add the parsley and black pepper.

Mix the mustards, vinegar and remaining oil together, then stir into the leeks and chickpeas and serve.

Bring a large pan of water to the boil. Plunge all the vegetables in it for 3 minutes. Drain immediately and place in a bowl.

Add the lemon zest and juice and combine with the extra virgin olive oil.

Italian-style green vegetables

200 g/7 oz. trimmed green beans
200 g/7 oz. tenderstem broccoli
100 g/3½ oz. young spinach leaves
grated zest and freshly squeezed
    juice of 1 lemon
1 mild fresh red chilli/chile,
    deseeded and finely chopped
    or 1 teaspoon crushed dried red
    chilli/hot pepper flakes
100 ml/6 tablespoons fruity extra
    virgin olive oil (Sicilian is best)
sea salt and freshly ground
    black pepper

SERVES 4–6

This very simple treatment of green vegetables is enduringly delicious, and I am thrilled to say so well received whenever I introduce it.

Bring a large pan of water to the boil. Plunge all the vegetables in it for 3 minutes. Drain immediately and place in a bowl.

Add the lemon zest and juice and combine with the extra virgin olive oil. Add the chilli/chile and season the dressing to taste.

Stir the dressing through the vegetables to coat.

Roman artichokes

4 medium globe artichokes
1 lemon, halved
3 bay leaves
150 ml/⅔ cup dry white wine

FOR THE DRESSING:
a large handful of fresh mint leaves,
    finely chopped
2 garlic cloves, finely chopped
3–4 tablespoons extra virgin
    olive oil
2 tablespoons white wine vinegar
sea salt and freshly ground
    black pepper

SERVES 4

Artichokes grow all over Italy, but the Lazio region, and Rome in particular, is especially renowned for its small, tender artichokes. Speciality dishes feature on restaurant menus throughout the capital during artichoke season. Try to buy young artichokes with long stalks, as these are tender and won't yet have developed much in the way of a choke. For this appetizer, the artichokes are best served warm.

Prepare the artichokes one at a time. Trim the base of the stalk at an angle, then peel the stem. Cut off the leaves about ½ cm/¼ in. from the top. Rub the cut surfaces with a lemon half. Now start peeling away the artichoke leaves, removing at least four layers, until the leaves begin to look pale. Spread the top leaves and use a teaspoon to scrape out the choke. Immerse the artichoke in a bowl of cold water with the other lemon half added (to prevent discolouration). Repeat to prepare the rest of the artichokes.

Place the bay leaves, lemon halves, wine and artichokes in a large saucepan and add enough cold water to cover (the artichokes should fit snugly in the pan). Bring to the boil, cover and simmer for about 30–35 minutes until the artichokes are tender. Drain the artichokes thoroughly.

To make the dressing, place the chopped mint leaves and garlic in a bowl with the oil and vinegar. Season to taste and whisk thoroughly to blend.

Arrange the artichokes upside down (with their stalks sticking up) on serving plates. Pour the dressing over the warm artichokes and serve.

Sweet Things

Italian almond apple cake

200 ml/¾ cup olive oil

225 g/1 cup plus 2 tablespoons light brown sugar

3 UK large/US extra large eggs

225 g/1¾ cups Italian '00' flour

1 teaspoon ground cinnamon

2½ teaspoons baking powder

½ teaspoon cream of tartar

600 g/1¼ lbs. tart dessert apples, peeled, cored and diced

100 g/⅔ cup raisins

75 g/¾ cup flaked/slivered almonds

grated zest of 2 unwaxed lemons

a 20-cm/8-in. springform cake pan, lined with baking parchment

SERVES 6–8

Born out of a glut of apples, this is the happy result of an experiment. The olive oil gives a light texture.

Heat the oven to 180°C (350°F) Gas 4.

Pour the olive oil into a bowl, add the sugar and beat until smooth with a hand-held electric mixer.

Add the eggs, one at a time, and beat until the mixture has increased in volume and resembles a thin mayonnaise.

Sift together the flour, cinnamon, baking powder and cream of tartar. Add these dry ingredients gradually to the oil mixture, folding them in with a metal spoon. Now add the apples, raisins, flaked/slivered almonds and lemon zest.

Spoon the batter into the prepared cake pan and bake in the preheated oven for 1 hour, until a skewer inserted in the cake comes out clean. Remove from the pan and leave to cool on a wire rack before serving.

The ultimate banana cake

100 g/²/₃ cup dried dates
240 g/2 cups Italian '00' flour
50 g/½ cup porridge/old-
    fashioned rolled oats
3 teaspoons baking powder
50 g/½ cup chopped pecans
1 teaspoon salt
60 g/⅓ cup brown sugar
120 ml/½ cup organic
    sunflower oil
200 g/¾ cup Greek yoghurt
75 ml/⅓ cup coconut milk
5 UK large/US extra large eggs
60 g/¼ cup clear honey
2 teaspoons vanilla extract
225 g/1 cup mashed bananas,
    super ripe (i.e. black)

*a 30-x 17-cm/12-x 6½-in. loaf
pan, oiled and base-lined
with baking parchment*

SERVES 12

Oil creates a winning texture in cakes – I hope the following recipe will convince you! I have had a lifetime's passion for bananas and a corresponding lifelong pursuit of the best banana recipes.

Preheat the oven to 180°C (350°F) Gas 4.

Soak the dates in boiling water for about 12 minutes.

Mix all of the dry ingredients together. Mix the wet ingredients together, except the bananas.

Drain the dates, remove the stones/pits and chop finely. Add the bananas and dates to the wet ingredients. Mix the dry and wet ingredients together until combined.

Spoon the mixture into the prepared pan and bake for 40 minutes until golden. If a skewer inserted into the loaf comes out clean, it is done. Cool on a wire rack, then serve.

- 15 g/½ oz. fresh yeast or 7 g/¼ oz. dried/active dry yeast
- 250 g/9 oz. strong white unbleached flour, plus extra for sprinkling
- ½ teaspoon sea salt
- 50 ml/3 tablespoons olive/coconut oil, plus extra to stretch and roll the dough
- finely grated zest of 1 lemon
- finely grated zest of 1 lime
- 2 teaspoons finely ground cardamom or 8 pods finely ground in a pestle and mortar
- 125 g/⅔ cup granulated white sugar
- vanilla icing/confectioners' sugar, to dust

2 baking sheets, oiled

MAKES 12–16

Lemon, lime & cardamom crackers

The lemon and lime zest here is the perfect partner to the perfumed cardamom. I like to serve these crackers with ice cream or soft fruit as the crunch of the crackers counterbalances their velvety texture.

Measure 50 ml/3 tablespoons warm water in a jug/measuring cup. Blend the fresh or dried/active dry yeast with a little of this water.

Sift the flour and salt together into a large bowl. Make a well in the centre and add the olive/coconut oil, along with half the lemon, lime, cardamom and sugar mix, the yeast liquid and some of the water. Mix together with a wooden spoon, gradually adding the remaining water, to form a soft dough.

Turn the dough out onto a lightly floured work surface and knead vigorously for 10 minutes until it is soft and satin-like (don't be afraid to add more flour). Place in a lightly oiled large bowl, then turn the dough around to coat with the oil. Cover the bowl with a clean dish towel and leave in a warm place for 1½ hours, or until the dough has doubled in size.

Preheat the oven to 200°C (400°F) Gas 6. Place the prepared baking sheets in the bottom of the oven.

Knock down the dough with your knuckles, then turn onto a lightly floured work surface. Knead for 2–3 minutes to knock out the air bubbles. Divide the dough in half. On a lightly floured work surface, roll out the pieces of dough very, very thinly, until 25–30 cm/10–12 in. in diameter. Lift each one onto a cold tray and top with the remaining lemon, lime, cardamom and sugar mix.

Carefully slide the prepared crackers off the cold tray directly onto the hot baking sheets and immediately bake in the oven for 12 minutes until golden and crisp. Dust with the vanilla icing/confectioners' sugar. When cold, crack them and enjoy!

Olive oil ice cream

This original recipe comes from Giovanni Fassi at the Palazzo del Freddo in Rome. It will be devoured by even the fiercest sceptic.

200 ml/¾ cup whole milk

140 g /¾ cup golden caster/ raw cane sugar

100 ml/½ cup double/heavy cream

5 UK large/US extra large egg yolks

160 ml/⅔ cup fruity olive oil

an ice cream maker (optional)

SERVES 4–6

Place the milk, sugar and cream in a pan and slowly bring to the boil. Make sure the sugar has dissolved. Remove from the heat and leave to cool. Whisk the egg yolks in a bowl with a balloon whisk.

When the milk and cream mixture is cool, add the egg yolks, a little at a time, to the pan over a low heat. You are aiming to create a custard. When the egg and milk mixture has thickened enough to coat the back of a spoon, remove it from the heat. Add the oil and whisk the mixture with a balloon whisk until well incorporated.

Place in an ice-cream maker and churn according to the manufacturer's instructions. Alternatively, place it in a metal tin in the freezer. You will need to remove the metal tin from the freezer and whisk the ice cream every hour and a half until it is smooth.

Cook's note: This recipe can also be made with coconut milk instead of cow's milk.

Homemade chocolate hazelnut spread

100 g/3½ oz. dark/bittersweet
  chocolate (minimum 70%
  cocoa solids)
100 ml/½ cup whole milk
75 g/1 cup ground hazelnuts,
  toasted
2 drops vanilla extract
125 ml/½ cup hazelnut oil
3 tablespoons double/heavy
  cream

MAKES ABOUT 500-G/1-LB.

When I was in Paris last summer, I had a focaccia coated in chocolate and hazelnut spread in a small artisan pizzeria near the Bastille market – it was utterly delicious. This set my imagination racing, and I decided to try making my own. I hope you enjoy it!

Melt the chocolate with the milk in a medium-size saucepan. Add the hazelnuts and vanilla extract, then the oil, little by little. When cool, add the cream. Transfer to a screw-top jar (or jars) and store in the refrigerator.

Please enjoy in as many ways as possible. It goes very well with focaccia, pancakes, muffins and crackers or simply spread on hot toast.

Index

Photography credits

Jan Baldwin *Pages 6-13, 22-26, 29, 30, 32-34, 37, 38, 41-44, 47, 48, 50-52*

Peter Cassidy *Page 2*

David Munns *Page 53*

William Reavell *Pages 31, 39*

Matt Russell *Pages 46, 49*

Ian Wallace *Pages 1, 3-5, 17, 19, 21, 45, endpapers*

Kate Whitaker *Page 27*

Clare Winfield *Pages 15, 18, 36*